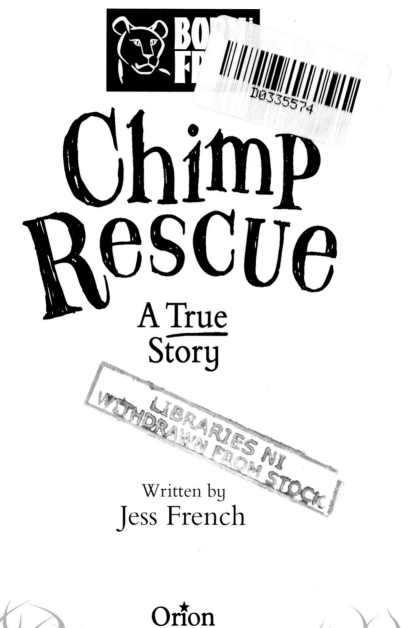

Chimp Rescue

A True Story

Written by
Jess French

Orion
Children's Books

ORION CHILDREN'S BOOKS

First published in Great Britain in 2016 by Hodder and Stoughton

1 3 5 7 9 10 8 6 4 2

A CIP catalogue record for this book is available from the British Library.

ISBN 978 1 5101 0054 1

Printed and bound in China

The paper and board used in this book are from
well-managed forestsand other responsible sources.

Orion Children's Books
An imprint of
Hachette Children's Group
Part of Hodder and Stoughton
Carmelite House
50 Victoria Embankment
London EC4Y 0DZ

An Hachette UK Company
www.hachette.co.uk

www.hachettechildrens.co.uk

Hello everyone,

Sometimes I feel that because there are so many
fearful things happening to elephants and tigers and
rhinoceroses and dolphins, we sometimes forget the
small animals. This, of course, doesn't mean they too
are not faced by all kinds of challenges from human

beings. On the contrary. At Born Free we care about them all and believe every creature, great and small, deserves to live as nature intended.

Our story began over 50 years ago, when my late husband, Bill Travers, and I travelled to Kenya to act in a film called 'Born Free'. It was inspired by a book of the same name, written by Joy Adamson, and was the extraordinary story of an orphaned lion cub, Elsa, which Joy and her husband George, raised and finally taught to become an independent wild lion. It was a remarkable achievement, and especially wonderful was the fact that Elsa remained close to her human friends, often visiting them and, finally, bringing her three wild-born cubs to meet them.

The experience of working with the Adamsons and several lions (none were 'trained') made a lasting impression on Bill and myself. In fact it changed our lives and in 1984, together with our eldest son Will, we started our own charity. We called it Zoo Check – as we strongly believed (and still do) that wild animals should live wild and free. Not kept captive or exploited by humans.

In 1991 we changed the name to The Born Free Foundation – our philosophy is unchanged but our work now includes trying to protect animals in the wild, our education programme called Global Friends, rescuing and caring for a variety of species, and campaigning for the end of killing animals for sport.

This story is about one of the very fascinating small animals. A little chimpanzee. As you will know, chimpanzees are the closest relative to humans. They share so many of the emotions we experience. Loneliness, joy, fear and family loyalty. So when you read Chinoise's story you will be able to share all her feelings in a very personal way. There are many vulnerable, little chimpanzees that need our help and I hope that the story of this beautiful, endearing animal will touch your heart as it has mine.

Virginia McKenna

Virginia McKenna
Actress and Founder Trustee, Born Free Foundation

BORN FREE AROUND THE WORLD

Animal Welfare

Born Free exposes animal suffering and fights cruelty.

Wild Animal Rescue

Born Free develops and supports many wild animal rescue centres.

Canada

United Kingdom

USA

South America

Conservation

Born Free protects wild animals in their natural habitat.

Communities and Education

Born Free works closely with communities who live alongside the projects we support.

Europe

Africa

China

India

Vietnam

Indonesia

This is the true story of a young chimpanzee called Chinoise. She was born in the forest of Cameroon, and then taken from her family to be used in the tourist industry. She almost gave up hope, until she was rescued by a charity supported by Born Free and everything began to change.

FACTFILE

Chinoise

- Born in the wild, in a forest in Cameroon
- Her favourite food is the Coula nut
- Enjoys cooling down by splashing in the pool
- Her best friend is Billy, another orphaned chimpanzee
- Likes to be the centre of attention
- Loves to be groomed but doesn't like grooming other chimpanzees
- Doesn't like bright lights or shouting

Learn a new ape fact
every time you see me.

Chapter One

Deep in the lush green forest of Cameroon, Central Africa, a baby chimpanzee was cradled in its mother's arms. Chinoise had been watching a group of young chimpanzees play. She wanted to join in, but at just a few months old, she wasn't yet strong enough to leave her mother's side.

For about the first six months of its life, a baby chimpanzee depends on its mother for everything. Chimpanzees provide their babies with food, warmth and protection. After five or six months, as the baby gets stronger, it will start to ride around on its mother's back, grabbing onto her hair to support itself.

FACT FILE

From this spot, Chinoise could see the whole group. Four chimpanzees sat in a row, grooming each other. They often had bits of dirt, plants or insects in their hair, which they needed help to remove. The chimpanzee at the front of the line was Chinoise's sister. She held out her arm and the next chimpanzee along parted the hair and picked out a small insect with her teeth. The older chimpanzees took it in turns to groom each other, but baby Chinoise was lucky. Her mother groomed her every day to keep her clean and to strengthen their bond.

Chimpanzees are primates in the group called 'hominidae' or 'great apes'. Other great apes in this group include orangutans, gorillas, bonobos and humans. Like all great apes, chimpanzees are large animals. They don't have tails and travel a lot by knuckle walking on the ground. The number of chimpanzees is rapidly decreasing because of threats such as poaching, deforestation and disease. Because of this, chimpanzees are endangered.

FACT FILE

A couple of young chimpanzees were still playing and chasing each other to the top branches of the trees. Sometimes they would collide in the clearing and wrestle in the dirt. The rest of Chinoise's group had wandered to another feeding spot for the day, but they would be back before dark. Adult chimpanzees mainly eat leaves and fruit, but sometimes they will eat other animals, from termites and beetle grubs to birds, bushpigs and monkeys. They also like to eat nuts and seeds. When the Coula tree was in season, Chinoise's family enjoyed nothing

more than feasting on its delicious nuts, breaking into the kernels by hitting them with stone hammers.

It was time for Chinoise's afternoon nap, but she was desperately trying not to close her eyes. She loved to watch as the older chimpanzees cracked open the nuts. They would lift the heavy stones high above their heads, then bring them down on the Coula branches. Chinoise still spent most of her time drinking milk from her mother, but occasionally she would be allowed to try a Coula nut.

It was once thought that humans were the only animals that were intelligent enough to use tools. Now we know that other primates, some birds and dolphins, use tools too. Chimpanzees use tools for lots of different things:

Ant or termite fishing: Dipping a stick into an ant or termite nest and feeding on them as they crawl and attach themselves to the end of it.

Drinking: Using crumpled leaves or moss as sponges to soak up water and drink from. Chimpanzees place these 'sponges' in their mouths and suck the water from them.

Nut cracking: Cracking nuts open with hammers made of stone or wood.

Hunting other animals: Chimpanzees will work together to hunt other animals such as monkeys, baby bushpigs and bushbuck.

A strong, old chimpanzee reached over to Chinoise. In his hand was a fresh Coula nut. She took it gratefully from her father and pushed it between her rubbery lips. He was the biggest and strongest of all the chimpanzees in her group, and the best nutcracker. Every day, he would spend hours patrolling the edges of her group's territory and protecting them from danger.

FACT FILE

Chimpanzees belong to one big group, 'the community', of up to one hundred chimpanzees. They often split up into small groups for feeding. The groups can consist of males and females of any age, but babies stay with their mothers until they are at least seven years old.

With a full belly, Chinoise couldn't keep her eyes open. Nowhere felt warmer and safer, so she buried her little pink hands into her mother's hair, and drifted off into a deep sleep.

Chimpanzees are territorial. Male chimpanzees from the group patrol the edges of their territory, to stop other chimpanzees from coming in.

FACT FILE

Chapter Two

A piercing noise woke Chinoise with a start. The chimpanzees in her group were all staring in the direction of the sounds. She didn't hear chimpanzees scream often, but it always meant something bad.

Chimpanzees rely heavily on communication to signal how they are feeling. One of the most distinctive calls is the 'pant-hoot', which is used socially for many different reasons. For example, when an individual finds food and wants to invite others to join him. The 'pant grunt' is used to show respect to dominant chimpanzees. The 'huu' is a noise of surprise or alarm. The 'hoo' is a whimper which babies make to ask their mothers for cuddles. The 'scream' is a loud noise, which travels over a long distance, which chimpanzees make when they are stressed or very scared.

FACT FILE

Chinoise heard some loud bangs. She was pulled towards her mother's tummy and wrapped protectively in her strong and hairy arms. Chinoise knew something was wrong – even her father looked frightened. Suddenly, a group of humans burst into the clearing. They held shiny black objects in their hands.

'Poaching' is the illegal hunting or killing of wild animals. Across Africa, chimpanzees are poached for their meat and for their heads, hands and feet, which are used as good luck charms or in traditional medicine. Poachers most commonly kill chimpanzees using guns, but some poachers still use traps, spears and harpoons.

Chinoise's family turned to run. Chinoise buried her face into her mother's hair and held on tightly with her tiny fists. There was a bang and her mother fell to the floor. Chinoise did not understand what was happening and did not lift her head. As long as she held on she knew she would be safe. She closed her eyes and nuzzled in closer.

FACT FILE

Adult chimpanzees are killed by poachers, but baby chimpanzees are too small to eat and therefore reach a higher price alive. Poachers take the baby chimpanzees from the forest and sell them as pets.

Chapter Three

When Chinoise opened her eyes, she was no longer holding her mother's coat. She was alone and trapped inside a coarse sack. She made a 'hoo' call to her mother, but there was no reply. She began to panic and scrambled about, trying to escape. A human kicked out at the wriggling body, and caught Chinoise hard in the stomach. She stopped struggling and whimpered quietly in pain.

The sack smelled strange and Chinoise was frightened.

She didn't know how long she had been asleep. It was impossible to tell the difference between night and day. She heard lots of strange noises, but no singing sunbirds or hooting scops owls to welcome the day. Chinoise wanted to see her mother, to slip into the nest and cuddle down for the night. But she was gone forever.

The strange noise that Chinoise could hear was the sound of a human market. It was mid-afternoon in central Douala. Families were browsing bright piles of fruit and vegetables, and stall holders were shouting the prices of their goods, battling each other to be heard. A group of teenage boys played tinny music from the stereo of a rusty old van as they watched women walk by in a rainbow of dresses. The smell of meat and acrid smoke mingled in the air. It was a strange place to illegally sell a baby chimpanzee and the bushmeat from its family.

Bushmeat' is the name given to meat that comes from wild animals, killed in their natural environment, in tropical areas. It is illegal to sell endangered animals, like chimpanzees, but it still happens.

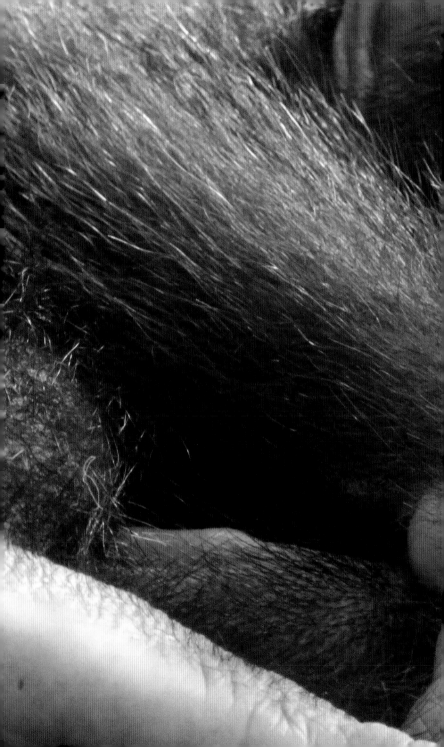

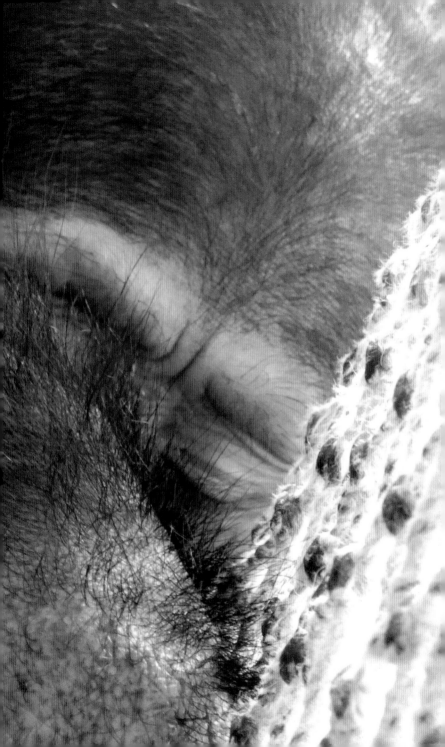

It wasn't long before Chinoise's sack was dragged to another area of the market. Every rock and stone bashed and bruised her body. Finally she was still again. There were even more new sounds. Parrots squawking, dogs barking and monkeys chattering. This didn't sound like her forest. Chinoise was confused. She had never been away from her mother before and had not yet learned to survive alone.

Chimpanzee babies are still dependent on their mothers for about the first 5 years of their lives. In the wild, even after a year, an infant won't wander further than a few metres from its mother.

The sack was flung open and a woman reached in. She pulled Chinoise out by her neck. Chinoise looked around with wide, scared eyes. There were rows of stalls and people rushing around everywhere like ants around an ants nest.

Before she could have a proper look around, Chinoise was thrust into the arms of the owner of a restaurant. This was the first time she had seen a human close up. She had long hair on her head, her muscles were small and covered with material and her face was round.

Chimpanzees and humans share more than 98% of their DNA. They are both extremely fast learners, use tools and pass on traditions from one generation to the next. Like humans, chimpanzees are capable of deceit and warfare.

Chinoise peered out over the woman's shoulder. She did not like this human world. It was loud, bright and foreign. She wondered what had happened to the rest of her family. Perhaps they were still in the forest, with its lush green leaves and delicious seeds. Chinoise was hungry. Her throat was scratchy and dry. She had not been given any food or water. Normally, she ate almost continuously throughout the day. Her stomach grumbled, but the humans didn't seem to notice.

FACT FILE

Anna Kucherova/Shutterstock.com

The restaurant owner passed some money to the people on the pet stall and Chinoise was pushed once again into the sack. A few stalls down, there were more illegal products. Rhino horn, for use in traditional medicine, decorative ivory pendants, leopard skins, dead turtles and at the end of the table, two chimpanzee hands, sold to be used as ashtrays.

Chimpanzee hands have four long fingers and a short thumb. Their feet have a type of thumb too, which allows them to grip with their feet as well as their hands.

Chapter Four

Chinoise was taken away from the market and carried to a restaurant. The smells were different here. There were not as many people but lots of buildings. A man approached. He held Chinoise's arms tightly to her sides while the woman fixed a rope around her neck.

When the rope was tight, they placed Chinoise in a cage. The bars were made of rusty steel and the floor was hard, grey concrete. There was barely enough room for Chinoise to stand. She sat down and started to pull on the rope around her neck. The man sat a few metres away, watching her. When he realised that she was trying to remove the rope, he shouted at her. She tried biting the rope, but this made him so angry that he threw a rock at her. It hit her hard on the shoulder. Chinoise whimpered.

There were no trees to protect her from the baking midday sun and her bones began to ache. Whenever the sun was too hot before, Chinoise's mother would climb down from the trees and sit in the shade. But in her new cage, there was no escape. Feeling frightened and weak from hunger and thirst, Chinoise fell asleep.

Many hours later, she woke to a human shaking her. It was the man that had thrown the rock. Everything was dark now. Night-time in the forest was for sleeping and snuggling into the safety of her mother's hair. In her tree nest she was safe from night-time predators like hyenas, less likely to be bitten by insects and much warmer than on the ground.

Here in the human world, the noises were louder at night. There seemed to be people walking around everywhere. The man who threw the rock pulled her from her cage and lifted her into his arms. He strode along the busy road, shouting. If people stopped, he would pass Chinoise to them. She

would cling tightly around the human's necks, for fear of being dropped to the floor. The people misunderstood this, and thought it was an act of love, not fear. Sometimes they would hug her and stroke her head. Sometimes they would poke or tickle her and pull her hair. The women would often squeal in her ear and look straight in her eyes, which were wide with fear. There was nearly always a flash of bright light.

FACT FILE

Like humans, chimpanzees have trichromatic vision, which means they see in three colours: red, green and blue. This helps them to spot which fruits are ripe and ready to eat.

The flashes of light came from cameras. Crowds of tourists would take Chinoise's picture every night. The man who threw the rock could earn a lot of money from charging people for photos with a baby chimpanzee. It is illegal to use a baby chimpanzee as a photo prop in this way, but the rules are rarely enforced.

They would often walk to areas where the streets thronged with people and the air was thick with smoke, music and singing. The people seemed loud and aggressive. Their breath had a strange, sour smell and their eyes were red and glazed.

When she was very frightened, Chinoise would make a face called a 'fear grimace'. She would look at the humans with her lips pulled far off her teeth. Often, the humans would make the same face back at her and shout, 'Look, she's smiling!' The most frightening thing of all was when the humans clapped their hands. In the wild, chimpanzees only clap their hands in threat displays, when they are trying to frighten other chimpanzees. When the humans did this, Chinoise would try to run away, but the man who threw the rock would grab her by the neck and shake her, or hit her on the head.

At the end of the night, Chinoise was thrown back into her cage and abandoned until the following evening. She tried to sleep, but the noises were so loud and her eyes were so bright from the flashes of light that she often lay awake for hours. The sun rose early and beat down relentlessly. All day she lay in the baking sun, often with no food or water. Sometimes the woman from the restaurant would throw her some rice. Chinoise didn't like the taste, but she was so hungry that she ate it ravenously. She felt constantly thirsty. When it rained, which it rarely did, Chinoise would try to catch water in her hands to drink. Her thick hair would hold the water for hours and for the rest of that day, she would gratefully suck water from it.

Some people think the 'fear grimace' looks like a human smile. It is the face that chimpanzees make when they are very scared. In the 'fear grimace', the mouth is wide open and the lips are pulled tight to bare both upper and lower teeth. Chimpanzees also have a 'play face', which they use when they are relaxed and want to enter into a game. In the 'play face', the upper lip covers the top teeth and the lower lip hangs loosely to show the bottom teeth.

Chinoise was tired, but throughout the day she would be disturbed by visitors who would come to look at her in her cage. Once, a group of young children beat her through the bars with a big stick. Day by day, her spirit began to break.

Chimpanzees sometimes drink water from holes in trees, particularly during the dry season. As this water is often too deep for them to reach just by using their mouths, they have invented clever solutions. They make sponges with moss or by chewing leaves so that they will soak up water.

Her routine did not vary very much. Every night, they would walk the streets and humans would flash bright lights in her eyes. Every day, she would try to sleep in the baking sun and grow thin and more dehydrated. After a while, Chinoise could barely lift her head.

Slowly, Chinoise was forgetting how to be a chimpanzee. The first few years of a chimpanzee's life are crucial. It is in this time that they learn to interact with other chimpanzees and to live in the forest. The sounds and smells of Chinoise's forest home were slowly fading into a distant memory, replaced by the stench and noise of this bustling human town.

Animals that are used as photography props are often injected with drugs or made to drink alcohol to keep them awake. The needles used to inject these drugs can spread dangerous diseases like hepatitis.

Chapter Five

After months of this, Chinoise believed it would be this way forever. She stopped paying attention to the humans that came to take pictures. All day, she rocked backwards and forwards in her cage and chattered her teeth. Worst of all, she had a constant headache that would not go away and her tummy always seemed to ache.

As a result of being forced to drink alcohol, chimpanzees in captivity can often develop liver problems.

The regular customers of the restaurant became so used to seeing the chimpanzee, they barely glanced in her direction any more. Chinoise did not recognise their faces, so she didn't notice when an unknown, kind-faced customer came to visit. The customer observed Chinoise rocking in her cage and chattering her teeth. She watched as Chinoise cowered from the scorching sun. She was angry that such a beautiful

and gentle creature was being kept in a cruel, steel cage. She knew something had to be done, and was desperate to help. Luckily, the customer knew of a famous sanctuary near Douala, called Limbe Wildlife Centre, which did amazing work, caring for rescued primates. Hoping for a better future for Chinoise, she called them to ask if they could help.

Limbe Wildlife Centre then called the Last Great Ape Organisation who immediately leapt into action. In order to rescue a chimpanzee, the charity needed proof of how and where it was being kept. So they sent their top investigator, Jean Pierre, to have a look around the restaurant. As soon as he arrived, Jean Pierre saw Chinoise sitting exactly where she always did. In her cage, in the baking sun, at the entrance to the restaurant. Jean Pierre knew that Chinoise must be rescued as quickly as possible.

Rescuing a chimpanzee is not a simple job. It needs to be carefully planned and there is lots of paperwork to be filled out. Jean Pierre set up a whole team of Wildlife Officials to prepare everything. This included a rescue car and a 'mission order', the official document that would allow Wildlife Officials to seize Chinoise.

On the 17th January 2014, Jean Pierre arrived at the restaurant with some staff from the Limbe Wildlife Centre and a group of Wildlife Officials. It had been a long drive, but now there was a buzz of energy in the air. Everyone knew that they only had one chance to get this right.

Jean Pierre was the first to approach the restaurant. As he drew closer, his heart sank. Something was wrong. Chinoise's cage no longer sat at the entrance to the restaurant and the chimpanzee was nowhere to be seen. Someone from the team must have warned the restaurant owner that they were coming.

Telling the Wildlife Officials to wait in the car, Jean Pierre went to investigate. He soon located the man who threw the rock and asked him where Chinoise had gone. The man explained that he had hidden her behind the restaurant. He offered to let Jean Pierre see the chimpanzee if he went and bought her some fruit.

When Jean Pierre returned with a ripe bunch of bananas, Chinoise was walked on a rope to the front of the restaurant. She reached hungrily for a banana, snatching it from Jean Pierre's hand. At that moment, the Wildlife Officials rushed over and began to question the man. Chinoise was confused by the commotion. She knew something unusual was happening, but she didn't realise her life was about to change.

The staff carried Chinoise away from the restaurant and over to their car. They gave her water to drink, then placed her in a soft, clean box. These people were gentle and spoke in quiet voices. Chinoise was driven to the Limbe Wildlife Centre. Limbe cares for fifteen different species of primates, including baboons, gorillas and chimpanzees. Although Chinoise was now out of immediate danger, this was only her first step along the road to recovery.

It has been illegal to sell endangered animals in Cameroon since 1994.

Chapter Six

The car journey was not painful and the box was lined with a soft blanket, but Chinoise was still frightened. She had no idea where they were taking her. All she knew was that humans had never been anything but bad news. When they finally arrived at the Centre, the staff opened the box to see a terrified face peering up at them.

They gently lifted Chinoise out of the box and carried her into a large and clean building. These humans seemed different, but she was scared and sometimes cried out in fear. They took Chinoise into a white room, with a strange, chemical smell in the air. The people in here wore blue gloves on their hands and white masks on their faces.

Chinoise was very sick but the veterinary team knew exactly how to help her. First, they needed to give her a full health check. The kindest way to do this was to give her a general anaesthetic, so she would sleep through all the tests.

One of the masked humans gave Chinoise some medicine to help her sleep deeply and peacefully. While she was under the anaesthetic, the vets looked into Chinoise's mouth, listened to her heart, took blood samples, read her temperature, weighed her, measured her, washed her and rubbed her dry with a towel. From her teeth and her body size, they guessed that she was around a year old.

FACT FILE

Looking at an animal's teeth is a great way to find out how old it is. Most mammals have baby teeth, followed by adult teeth, and these adult teeth appear in a specific order, usually at a specific age. Chimpanzees don't get their canine teeth – the sharp and pointy ones – until they are a year old.

They discovered that she had a high fever from

an infection, was badly dehydrated and had a huge and swollen liver. The vets gave her some fluids to make her feel better and some injections to reduce her fever. Then they vaccinated her, to prevent her getting nasty diseases in the future.

When Chinoise's health check was over, she was laid on a pile of soft towels to wake up in her own time. As she came round, she blinked her eyes slowly. She was confused. She had no idea where this place was. She noticed that her hair was clean and her headache had gone, but she felt tired and hungry. A short while later, one of the team brought over something to eat. Fresh leaves, fruit and seeds from the forest. What a feast! Chinoise had only eaten scraps of human food and occasional bananas for the whole time she was in captivity. She finished the bowl of food gratefully.

Wild chimpanzees learn which leaves and fruit in the forest are safe to eat by watching their mothers. Once a young chimpanzee is weaned, it will copy its mother by eating what she eats.

Chinoise was kept in the quarantine section of Limbe Wildlife Centre for 90 days. She was monitored to ensure that she did not have any infectious diseases, which could harm the other primates. During this time she was nursed back to full health, and treated for liver disease and infection. She was also fed lots of natural, healthy food.

FACT FILE

Quarantine means keeping an animal on its own when it first arrives to a new place. This is to stop it spreading any infectious diseases that it may be carrying. Quarantine is particularly important in chimpanzees because they can spread diseases to humans.

Chinoise was still frightened of humans. But the nurses looking after her were dedicated, persistent and kind. Every day, they would bring her fresh food and try to play with her. They would hide delicious treats like honey inside hollow wooden logs and show her how to stick her fingers inside to pull it out. In the beginning, Chinoise would hide away at the back of her cage and sit in silence, rarely crying, or making any noise at all. For the first month, she continued to rock backwards and forwards, not understanding where she was and terrified by her previous experiences. But little by little, Chinoise began to trust these humans.

One day, after two months in quarantine, Chinoise was brave enough to sit down right beside the person who had come to play with her, and allow him to stroke her on the arm. Her trust was building.

Chapter Seven

After three months in quarantine, Chinoise looked much better. She was healthy and strong and her eyes were bright and full of life. She no longer sat quietly in the back of her cage, but at the front, calling excitedly for her food when it arrived. Chinoise passed her quarantine, showing no signs of infectious disease and was ready to move onto the next stage.

On the last morning of her quarantine, Chinoise climbed into the arms of the human who had brought her food. She was now much less fearful of people, and seemed to enjoy spending time with the Centre's staff. Chinoise had never been out of the quarantine centre before, but today they walked outside into the bright sunshine. She looked around nervously.

As they approached the trees, Chinoise began to notice a range of familiar sights and sounds.

She looked up. The leaves of the tree cast a welcome shadow over her face. These were the same trees her mother had climbed with her every evening, to build a sleeping nest and snuggle down for the night. She sniffed at the air. It smelled warm and earthy. A bird sang loudly overhead.

She looked around at the trees and plants, trying to remember which trees were good to eat, which ones produced bitter fruit and which ones gave the best shade. It took a while before she spotted the three hunched figures, sitting in a patch of shade. She stared in stunned silence. She would recognise those hairy black features anywhere. They were other chimpanzees.

The human placed Chinoise on the floor and walked away, leaving her alone with the other chimpanzees. After such a long time, Chinoise could not remember how to act around them. She hid in a corner, watching quietly. The other chimpanzees played together, rolling around on the ground and swinging on the climbing frame in their enclosure. Sometimes they would run close to Chinoise and she would shuffle back out of the way.

FACT FILE

Chimpanzees are extremely social animals. They rely on their group for safety and support. Knowing how to act in social situations is very important.

All of the chimpanzees in the enclosure were also rescued orphans. They played together effortlessly and looked so much like the wild chimpanzees in the forest that it was hard to believe that they had once forgotten how to act like chimpanzees too. After a morning of play, the humans brought the chimpanzees some Coula nuts. They immediately set about cracking the nuts with stones, to get at the fruit inside, just as her family had done in the forest.

FACT FILE

Different groups of chimpanzees use tools in different ways. Each group has its own set of tools and methods of using them. Young chimpanzees learn these techniques from watching their mothers and other members of the community.

The nearest chimpanzee to Chinoise was called Billy. She looked over as she cracked her stone onto a nut. Billy had been rescued in an even worse state than Chinoise. She was locked away and starved, with only a puppy for company. When Billy arrived at Limbe, she had a broken jaw and a viral infection.

Now Billy was thriving. She had learned how to act around other chimpanzees, and although she was frightened of male chimpanzees, she loved to make friends with other young females.

Female chimpanzees stay in the group they were born into for roughly ten years, then move to a new community. Male chimpanzees stay in the group they were born into for their whole lives.

Chinoise was aware that Billy was staring at her, but she would not return her gaze. Billy only wanted to welcome Chinoise into her nursery group, which was currently made up of five chimpanzees, Madame, Lolo, Ghaa, Yabien and Billy.

They had all come to Limbe Wildlife Centre in similar circumstances to Chinoise. Yabien had been chained tightly to a concrete wall for over two years, and when she arrived was so distressed that she would do nothing but rock backwards and forwards. Lolo and Ghaa had both received gunshot wounds when their families were killed. And Madame had injured her wrist so badly that she could no longer use it. Chinoise had never properly learned how to make chimpanzee friends, and was scared to let Billy come close to her. When Billy edged towards Chinoise across the dry, cracking grass, Chinoise recoiled and let out a small cry.

It would take some time for Chinoise to trust the other chimpanzees. Almost all of her childhood so far had been spent isolated and miserable and she had not seen any of her own species for nearly a year. Until Chinoise was integrated with the group she would only spend the daylight hours in the nursery. At night she would go back to quarantine, where she felt safe.

As time passed, Chinoise grew more and more excited about going to the nursery. She would watch the other chimpanzees intently, listen to their calls and imitate their faces. Every day, Billy would come a little closer and try to interact with Chinoise.

One evening, as the sun was setting in the late summer sky, Chinoise allowed Billy to approach her. Shaking with nerves, she turned her back to

Billy. Gently, Billy began to search her hair for flies and other insects. The feeling of being groomed was so familiar, it was as if she was in the forest with her family. Whenever Billy found a bug in Chinoise's hair, she would squash it with her nimble fingers then grab it with her rubbery lips, grunting contentedly. Chinoise closed her eyes, enjoying the cool of the shade and the sunbirds singing above her. She was beginning to remember.

Chapter Eight

In the dry season, Cameroon is scorched by soaring temperatures. The winds swirl desert dust across the sky, covering it in a crimson haze.

The Harmattan is a trade wind that blows from the Sahara, bringing desert dust across Western Africa.

Luckily for the animals at Limbe Wildlife Centre, the staff keep their enclosure pools topped up with fresh water. If you visit Limbe in the dry season, that is where you will find Chinoise! Splashing about in the nursery pool, and jumping in and out with great gusto.

She loves playing in the water, especially in the afternoons, when the baking sun is at its fiercest, and she now lives in the nursery full-time.

FACT FILE

Chimpanzees are recognisable by their faces, just like humans.

The six orphaned chimpanzees have formed their own little family. Chinoise is their new baby and has rapidly become the centre of attention. Yabien and Billy love to carry her around, and groom and comfort her. She also spends lots of time playing with Ghaa, Lolo and Madame. But Chinoise is very independent! When food arrives, she tears across the nursery enclosure to make certain that she gets first pick of the leaves and fruit. Her favourite treat is still the Coula nut. And with a little help from her new friends, she is slowly learning to crack them open for herself.

Chinoise will never be able to be released back into the wild. Deforestation is depleting her natural habitat at such an alarming rate, that it is very difficult to find space for rescued chimpanzees in the wild.

Around the world, every minute, 20 football fields' worth of forest is cut down.

FACT FILE

Not only that, but Chinoise has missed the crucial early years of learning, which she should have received from her mother and close family. She would not know how to survive in the wild, how to hide away from predators, how to build a night nest, or which foods to eat. The liver disease that Chinoise contracted as a result of her conditions in captivity may also need lifelong veterinary care. But Chinoise has a new family now, and will live out her years with friends, food and all the medical attention that she needs thanks to the efforts of The Last Great Ape Organisation, Limbe Wildlife Centre and the Born Free Foundation, who provide support for their amazing work and Chinoise's care. At last she is safe.

As the huge red sun sets behind its veil of desert dust, Chinoise hops out of the pool and into a hammock between the trees. She motions Billy to join her, and they settle down for the night.

As the birds sing and darkness falls, Chinoise falls happily to sleep, wrapped tightly in her new friend's arms.

Great Apes in the Wild
CHIMPANZEES AND BONOBOS

Chimpanzees and bonobos are the apes most similar to people in their biology and behaviour. They have very complex social relationships and sophisticated systems of communication.

ABOUT CHIMPANZEES:

Estimated population:
 150, 000 – 250, 000

Live across Equatorial Africa

Population status: Endangered

ABOUT BONOBOS:

Estimated population: 30, 000 – 50, 000

Live in the Democratic Republic of Congo

Population status: Endangered

WHAT THREATENS CHIMPANZEES AND BONOBOS?

Hunting is one of the greatest threats facing chimpanzees and bonobos. They are hunted by poachers for many reasons- to be sold as bush meat, to use their babies to sell as pets and to use their body parts as souvenirs and in traditional medicine. Deforestation is also a huge problem, not only because it decreases the amount of land available for chimpanzees and bonobos to live in, but also because logging allows hunters better access to the forest. In order to take logs from the forest, new roads are built and these roads can be used by poachers to enter deep into the forest.

Orangutans

These big, orange apes live high up in the trees of South East Asia. They are almost completely arboreal, which means they spend almost all their time off the forest floor. Orangutans are the least sociable of the Great Apes, and usually live alone, only coming together to mate.

Gabriela Insuratelu/Shutterstock.com

About Bornean orangutans:

Estimated Bornean Orangutan population: 50,000

Live in Borneo, Indonesia and Malaysia

Population status: Endangered

ABOUT SUMATRAN ORANGUTANS:

Estimated Sumatran Orangutan population: 7,300

Live in Sumatra, Indonesia

Population status: Critically Endangered

WHAT THREATENS WILD ORANGUTANS?

The biggest threat to wild orangutans is the conversion of their native forest into palm oil plantations. Palm oil is used in approximately half of the products we use every single day as it is cheap and has a huge range of uses. Natural forest contains lots of plants and trees and supports many different animals. When only one plant is grown in an area, such as palm oil, it can no longer support such diversity. Not only do palm oil plantations provide a poor habitat for orangutans to live in, farmers often shoot or burn orangutans that they see feeding on their crops. Orangutans are also killed to take their babies for the pet trade.

Gorillas

Gorillas are the biggest of the great apes, with males weighing almost 200kg! The females often weigh half this, and live in big groups, with one silverback male. They spend most of their time eating and sleeping as the majority of their diet is made up of leaves.

ABOUT WESTERN LOWLAND GORILLAS:

Estimated Western Lowland Gorilla population: probably less than 95, 000

Live across Central Africa

Population status: Critically Endangered

ABOUT EASTERN LOWLAND GORILLAS:

Estimated Eastern Lowland Gorilla population: Unknown, less than 4, 000

Live in Eastern Democratic Republic of Congo

Population status: Endangered

ABOUT CROSS RIVER GORILLAS:

Estimated Cross River Gorilla population: 250–300

Live around the Nigeria / Cameroon border

Population status: Critically endangered

ABOUT MOUNTAIN GORILLAS:

Estimated Mountain Gorilla population: 880

Live in the Virunga Volcano region and Bwindi National Park

Population status: Critically Endangered

WHAT THREATENS WILD GORILLAS?

Gorilla habitat is rapidly being destroyed by logging, mining and oil exploration. These industries also allow poachers to travel into gorilla territory and to introduce devastating diseases. Gorillas are particularly susceptible to the Ebola virus. When a group of gorillas is infected with Ebola, up to 95% of those individuals are likely to die. Gorillas are also killed for bushmeat, body parts for use in medicine or as magic charms for use in the pet trade.

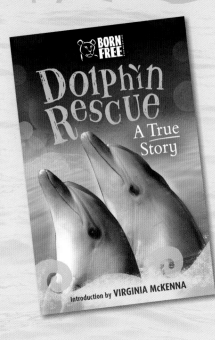

Read all
the rescue
stories

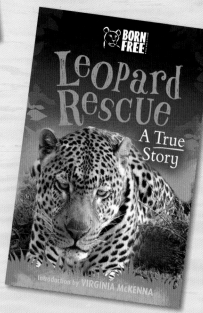

Keep Wildlife in the Wild

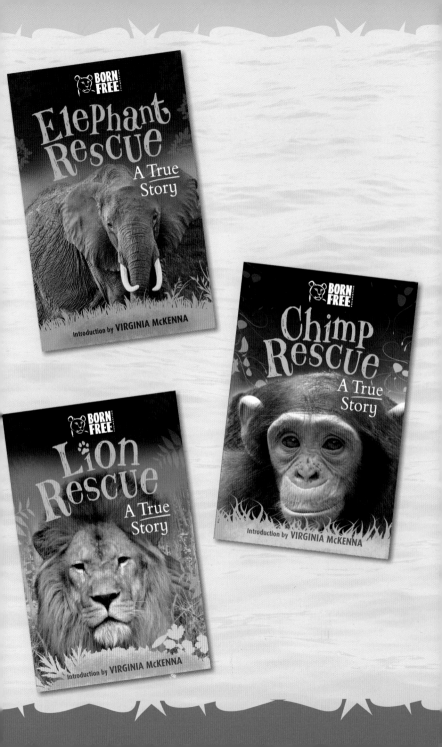

Go wild with Born Free

Welcome to the Born Free Foundation, where people get into animals and go wild! Our wildlife charity takes action all around the world to save lions, elephants, gorillas, tigers, chimps, dolphins, bears, wolves and lots more.

If you're wild about animals visit
www.bornfree.org.uk
to find out more, join our free kids' club WildcreW or adopt your own animal.

Keep Wildlife in the Wild